fail fail again fail better

Also by Pema Chödrön

Books

How to Meditate
Practicing Peace
When Things Fall Apart
Start Where You Are
The Places That Scare You
The Wisdom of No Escape
Taking the Leap
Living Beautifully with Uncertainty and Change
No Time to Lose

Audio

Walking the Walk
How to Meditate
Unconditional Confidence
No Time to Lose
Getting Unstuck
Pure Meditation

fail
fail again
fail better

Pema Chödrön
foreword by Seth Godin

SOUNDS TRUE
BOULDER, COLORADO

Sounds True
Boulder, CO 80306

© 2015 Pema Chödrön
Foreword © Seth Godin

Sounds True is a trademark of Sounds True, Inc.

Cover and book design by Lisa Kerans
Cover image © Shutterstock.com

Printed in the United States of America

Library of Congress Cataloging-in-Publication Data
Chödrön, Pema.
Fail, fail again, fail better : wise advice for leaning in to the unknown /
Pema Chödrön.
    pages cm
ISBN 978-1-62203-531-1
1. Failure (Psychology) 2. Uncertainty. 3. Self-actualization (Psychology)
I. Title.
BF575.F14C474 2015
158.1—dc23
                                    2015003010

Ebook ISBN 978-1-62203-557-1

10 9 8 7 6 5 4 3 2 1

Ani Pema Chödrön was invited
to give the commencement address to
the 2014 graduating class of Naropa
University in Boulder, Colorado.

This book contains the full text of that
speech, plus a Q & A with Tami Simon,
publisher of Sounds True, on the topic
of failure, regret, and leaning in to
the beautiful mystery of life.

To my granddaughter Alexandria—
with love and appreciation

"Ever tried. Ever failed. No matter. Try again. Fail again. Fail better."

—Samuel Beckett

CONTENTS

FORWARD

My first book was published thirty years ago. Finished manuscript in hand, I eagerly sent it off to a famous author, a respected entrepreneur whom I had met a few months earlier. "Would you be willing to write the forward to my new book?" I asked. My editor and my co-author were both counting on my connection to this man to transform our book into the bestseller we hoped it might become.

Two days later, the response showed up in my mailbox. "I would have been happy to contribute to your new book, Seth, but since you spelled 'foreword' wrong, I'm afraid I have to pass."

As a first-time author, everything was at stake, and this very personal, very careless failure resonated with me for years to come. I had blown it, really and truly.

A few years ago, I began to think of this differently. What Andy had inadvertently taught me is that "forward" is far more powerful and important than "foreword" ever could be.

In the years that followed that book, I got more than a thousand rejections to the book proposals I sent to publishers. I launched projects that didn't work the way I hoped they would. I wrote blog posts that didn't resonate and spread, told stories on stage that didn't hit their mark. All in an effort to go forward.

To use a phrase from Pema Chödrön, to go forward is to give up on "getting all the frogs in the bowl."

Perhaps your job in life, your purpose, is to get all the frogs in a bowl and keep them there.

As soon as we get a few frogs in the bowl, they jump out, and we have to start all over again.

Wouldn't it be great, we wonder, if we could just find stability, if everything would work out just the way we hope, if finally, finally all the frogs were in the bowl?

And then what would happen?

If you've signed up for the job of frog trainer, it's worth understanding that the only way to actually end up with an entire bowl of stable frogs (every single frog) is to euthanize the frogs. And where's the joy in a bowl of dead frogs?

No, the jumping frogs aren't merely an unfortunate hassle for the frog tamer. They are, in fact, the entire point.

James Carse, author of *Finite and Infinite Games,* taught us about the infinite game, the game that's not played to win (like soccer or the stock market) but the game that's played to be played. Every move in the infinite game is designed to help our partners, to keep the game moving, to enable the dance to keep moving.

In this powerful essay about failure, our teacher Pema Chödrön connects the frogs and the game. She helps us see, once and for all, that failure is part of success, and that both are essential elements in forward motion, in playing the infinite game.

The generous and irrepressible Pema Chödrön has given us here, in just a few pages, a chance to go forward. We all know that the mire and the muck is just outside our door, waiting to get us stuck, yet Pema teaches us to dance instead. Dance while the frogs continue to jump.

—Seth Godin

fail fail again fail better

The Naropa University
2014 Commencement Address

I said to my granddaughter in her freshman year, "If you graduate, I will give the talk."

So, apparently, she is graduating.

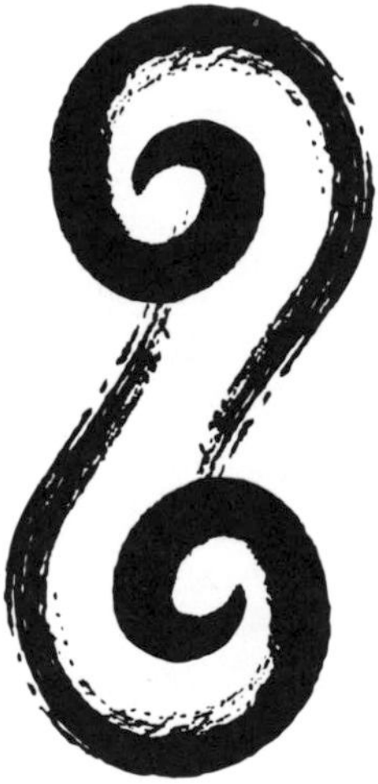

I have never given a graduation speech
before. When I asked for advice, they said,
"Short. Keep it short."

I thought a lot about what would be helpful
to all of you who are about to go out there,
not knowing what is going to happen. And
you could say that this is true for all of us.

No one ever knows what is going to
happen next.

But these transition times—between
something being set (like being a student
and coming back to that each year) and
things being uncertain—are times of
enormous potential.

Anything is possible.

So, now what? Will you be able to get a job?

Big question.

What's it going to be like to try to support
yourself without any help from anybody?

That's a good question.

I was shown a cover of a book from the 1980s, and the book was called, *What Are You Going to Do after College?* And on the cover of it was this man graduating in cap and gown, and he was looking out, full of promise, but he was stepping into a vast void, a spiraling-downward vortex. And I thought, gosh, that is a pretty accurate picture of what it is like to graduate—even more now than in the 80s.

It reminds me of when I was first taught
to teach. It was here in Boulder, actually.
I was working at what's now the Shambhala
Center, and I was being taught how to teach,
as many of us were. And the instructions
I received were to prepare well, know
your subject, and then go in there with
no note cards.

Honestly, that is the best advice for life:
no note cards.

Just prepare well and know what you want to do. Give it your best, but you really don't have a clue what's going to happen.

And note cards have limited usefulness.

So when Naropa asked me for the topic of my talk, I decided not to give it to them because I thought if I did, they wouldn't let me do it!

My talk is inspired by a quote from Samuel Beckett that goes like this. He knew something about waiting with no note cards!

The quote is "Fail. Fail again. Fail better."

I thought if there is one skill that is not
stressed very much, but is really needed,
it is knowing how to fail well.

The fine art of failing.

There is a lot of emphasis on succeeding.
And whether we buy the hype or not, we all
want to succeed, especially if you consider
success as "it works out the way I want it to."
You know it feels good in the gut and in the
heart because it worked out. So failing by
that definition is that it didn't work out the
way you wanted it to.

And [failing] is what we don't usually get a lot
of preparation for.

I think in college or university, if there is one thing that prepares you for having some idea of how to work with the rawness of things not working out the way you want them to, it would be contemplative education. As I listened to all the other speakers, it reinforced what I already thought was true, which is that you have gotten a lot of instruction and encouragement and support for feeling how things impact you and not just going down the tubes with it, but actually taking responsibility for what is happening to you and having some tools about how to work with painful feelings, raw feelings.

So fail, fail again, fail better. It's like how to get good at holding the rawness of vulnerability in your heart.

Or how to get good at "welcoming the unwelcome." That is a quote from the founder of Passage Works, which brings contemplative education into elementary schools.

Welcoming the unwelcome.

If you even remember the Beckett quote, I think it's what will help you more than anything else in the next six months, the next year, the next ten years, the next twenty years, for as long as you live, until you drop dead.

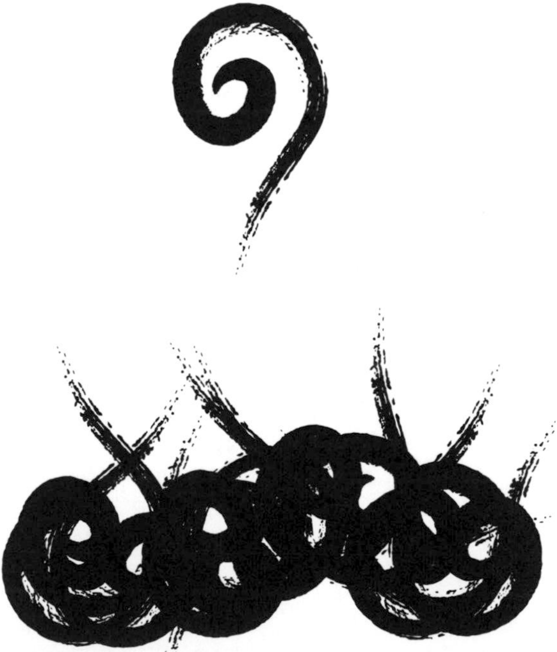

So how to fail?

Well, one of the things I want to say about failure is that it feels very raw.

I think the most significant thing about it is that we usually think of it as something that happens to us from the outside, right? We can't get in a good relationship or we are in a relationship that ends painfully or we can't get a job. Or we are fired from the job we have. Or we don't get the grades we want, or any number of not getting things the way we want them to be that we think of as failure, as something that happens to us.

There are usually two ways that we deal with that. We either blame it on somebody else or some other—the organization, our boss, or partner, whatever.

We move away from the rawness, of holding the rawness of vulnerability in our heart, by blaming it on the other.

The other really common thing, which is probably inherent in whatever approach we take, is that we feel really bad about ourselves and label ourselves

"a failure."

We have this feeling that there is something fundamentally wrong with us—something basically wrong with us.

I think this is what we need a lot of help with: this feeling that there is something wrong with us, that *we* actually are a failure because of the relationship not working out, the job not working out, or whatever it is, botched opportunities, doing something that flops.

Heartbreak of all kinds.

One of the ways to sort of pull yourself up or help yourself to hold this is to begin to question what is really happening when there is a failure.

So someone gave me a quote, something from James Joyce's *Ulysses,* where Joyce wrote about how failure can lead to discovery. And he actually didn't use the word "failure"; he used the word "mistake," as in making a mistake. He said that mistakes can be "the portals of discovery."

In other words, mistakes are the portal to creativity, to learning something new, to having a fresh look on things.

It's a little hard to tell what's a failure and what's just something that is shifting your life in a whole new direction. And I will use me as an example of that. The worst time in my life was when I felt like the greatest failure, and this had to do with a second failed marriage.

I had never experienced such rawness

and vulnerability

and pain

as during that particular groundless, rug-pulled-out kind of experience.

And I really felt bad about myself.

It took me a good three years to actually make the transition from just wanting to go back to the solid ground of what I had known before to having the willingness to actually go forward into a whole brand-new life.

It was the worst time of my life, and it resulted in a really good life that has a lot of happiness and well-being, a profound well-being pervading my life. And so even though that inner transformation hadn't occurred by conventional success—you know, the guidelines of conventional success—it resulted in me becoming a best-selling author!

There is this Tibetan story that takes place in rural Tibet in the eighteenth or nineteenth century, and in the story there is an older couple, a man and woman. They have two things that are extremely precious to them: their horse and their son.

The reason the horse and the son are so precious to them is because they need them to survive and farm the land and to tend to everything that needs to be done. The horse does a lot of work, and the son does a lot of work. They live in a small village, and their horse, this well-trained stallion, runs away, so the wife and all the people in the village say, "OMG! This is definitely the worst thing that could happen. This is terrible. This is *the worst thing*."

And the old man says,

"Maybe yes, maybe no."

The very next day the stallion returns with a mare. That's why he ran away. So he returns with a mare, and now they have two horses. And the wife and all the people in the village say, "Wow! This is the best thing that could have possibly happened. This is such good fortune. Now you have these two horses. This is amazing! This is so wonderful!"

And the old man says,

"Maybe yes, maybe no."

The next day, the son decides that he needs to tame the mare because she is a wild horse, and in trying to tame her, he gets thrown and he breaks his leg.

You can imagine what the wife and the rest of the village said. "Oy vey. Why us? This is the worst thing that could happen. This is a catastrophe."

And you know by now what the old man said:

"Maybe yes, maybe no."

The next day, the army comes in and takes away all the able-bodied men to fight in the war. The wife and the villagers really haven't still gotten the message that I am trying to get through to you; they are still just blown around by outer circumstances. When circumstance goes up, they are overjoyed. When it goes down, they feel their life is over.

But the old man says,

"Maybe yes, and maybe no."

That is as far as the story goes, but you can imagine it going on to infinity.

So when my second marriage ended, I could have said—and well, I actually would say it to anyone who would listen—"This is the worst time of my life; my life is over. I am going to die," and so on. And if the old man had been there, he would have said, "Maybe yes, and maybe no."

Getting back to the main point, which centers on this question:

Can you allow yourself to feel what you feel when things don't go the way you want them to? When things don't go the way you hoped and wished for and longed for them to go?

Sometimes you experience failed expectations as heartbreak and disappointment, and sometimes you feel rage. Failure or things not working out as you'd hoped doesn't feel good; that's for sure. But at that time, maybe instead of doing the habitual thing of labeling yourself a "failure" or a "loser" or thinking there is something wrong with you, you could get curious about what is going on. And really this is where I think your education will come in handy. If you can just remember the old man and what he had to say about what is happening, you'll remember that you never know where something will lead.

Getting curious about outer circumstances and how they are impacting you, noticing what words come out and what your internal discussion is, this is the key.

If there is a lot of "I am bad; I am terrible," somehow just notice that and maybe soften up a bit. Instead say, "What am I feeling here? Maybe what is happening here is not that I am a failure—I am just hurting. I am just hurting."

This is what human beings have felt from the beginning of time. If you want to be a full, complete human being, if you want to be genuine and not pretend that everything is either one way or the other way but you can hold the fullness of life in your heart, then this is the opportunity when you can get curious about what is going on and listen to the storylines. And you don't buy the storylines that blame it on everybody else. And you don't buy the storylines that blame it on yourself either.

How many here have seen the new Beyoncé music video? Track one is called "Pretty Hurts," and wow, does Beyoncé capture on this music video what it feels like to feel like a failure, right? It is so raw. She puts it all out there, and you figure she must know what it feels like to feel like a failure, even though she is a roaring success and everything is going her way.

Beyoncé couldn't have made that video if she hadn't had some real experience of knowing what it felt like to fail to the degree that the woman in "Pretty Hurts" felt. So sometimes you can take rawness and vulnerability and turn it into creative poetry, writing, dance, music, song. Artists have done this from the beginning of time. Turn it into something that communicates to other people, and out of this raw and vulnerable space, communication really happens.

This is the thing: I have been in this space of feeling like a failure a lot of times, and so I feel like a pro in this space actually. And I used to be like anybody else when I was in this space. I'd just kind of close down, and there was no awareness or curiosity or anything.

I carried a lot of habitual reactivity of trying to get out of that space of feeling like I had failed. And then as years went by (and meditation had a big part to play in this), I began to get to the place where I really do become curious when I find myself once again in this space that you can call failing—the kind of raw visceral feeling of having blown it or failed or having gotten something wrong or having hurt someone's feelings, whatever it is.

And so I can tell you that it is out of this space that real genuine communication with other people starts to happen, because it's a very unguarded, wide-open space where when you look out your eyes—unless you are getting into the blaming yourself or blaming others—you can go beyond the blame and just feel the bleedingness of it, the raw-meat quality of it.

You can't describe it, but I bet everybody knows what I am talking about. And so in that space, communication with others and all of life happens, and my experience is that it's from that space that our best part of ourselves comes out. It's in that space—when we aren't masking ourselves or trying to make circumstances go away—that our best qualities begin to shine.

The alternative is that out of that space of failure comes addictions of all kinds—addictions because we are not wanting to feel it, because we want to escape, because we want to numb ourselves.

Out of that space comes aggression, striking out, violence at others.

Out of that space comes a lot of ugly things. And yet out of that very same space of vulnerability and rawness and the feeling of failure can come our best human qualities of bravery, kindness, the ability to really care about each other, the ability to reach out to each other.

So I thought I would tell you this little story about Naropa University's founder, Chögyam Trungpa Rinpoche, and my very first one-on-one interview with him. This interview occurred during the time when my life was completely falling apart, and I went there because I wanted to talk about the fact that I was feeling like such a failure and so raw.

But when I sat down in front of him, he said, "How is your meditation?"

I said, "Fine."

And then we just started talking, superficial chatter, until he stood up and said, "It was very nice to meet you," and started walking me to the door. In other words, the interview was over.

And so at that point, realizing the interview was over, I just blurted out my whole story:

My life is over.
I have hit the bottom.
I don't know what to do.
Please help me.

And here is the advice Trungpa Rinpoche gave me. He said, "Well, it's a lot like walking into the ocean, and a big wave comes and knocks you over. And you find yourself lying on the bottom with sand in your nose and in your mouth. And you are lying there, and you have a choice. You can either lie there, or you can stand up and start to keep walking out to sea."

So, basically, you stand up, because the "lying there" choice equals dying.

Metaphorically lying there is what a lot of us choose to do at that point. But you can choose to stand up and start walking, and after a while another big wave comes and knocks you down.

You find yourself at the bottom of the ocean with sand in your nose and sand in your mouth, and again you have the choice to lie there or to stand up and start walking forward.

"So the waves keep coming," he said. "And you keep cultivating your courage and bravery and sense of humor to relate to this situation of the waves, and you keep getting up and going forward."

This was his advice to me.

Trungpa then said, "After a while, it will begin to seem to you that the waves are getting smaller and smaller. And they won't knock you over anymore."

That is good life advice.

It isn't that the waves stop coming; it's that because you train in holding the rawness of vulnerability in your heart, the waves just appear to be getting smaller and smaller, and they don't knock you over anymore.

A lot of you are aware of the [National Climate Assessment] report that came out about three weeks ago or so. It was a bipartisan climate change report that said three main things:

One, climate change is really happening (for the doubters).

Two, there are certain things that we can do to help it not get worse.

Three, there are some things that are not fixable.

You are entering into a world where there are a lot of things that aren't fixable. Whether they are at the level of climate change or things that happen to you in your life, and so this teaching on "fail, fail again, fail better" could come in really handy when you begin to feel knocked down by these great big waves and you begin to train in holding the vulnerability—the rawness and the vulnerability in your heart—knowing first of all it is the beginning of something really fresh and new in your life, turning you in a whole different direction. And second, it is making you braver and stronger and more there for other people, and it will bring out your best human abilities.

Thank you very much.

LEANING IN TO THE SHARP POINTS

A Conversation on Failure
with Pema Chödrön and Tami Simon

*I was thrilled when Pema Chödrön agreed to do
a follow-up interview to her 2014 commencement speech at Naropa University. The interview
was scheduled several months in advance, and
we arranged for it to take place in a retreat
cabin in Crestone, Colorado, approximately a
four-hour drive from Boulder. I'd been there
once before.*

*Ani Pema (as she is called by many friends
and students, "Ani" being a prefix meaning
"Aunt" that is often used in Tibetan Buddhism
to address a woman who is a nun) rarely gives
interviews. Knowing this and greatly valuing this
opportunity, I was determined to set out quite
early on the day of the interview.*

Teaming up with a Sounds True engineer, we drove to Crestone, and as planned, arrived thirty minutes early to the driveway to Ani Pema's cabin. At least we thought it was the driveway. A few minutes before the scheduled interview time, we drove up the driveway only to find that we were driving on a narrow, winding uphill road that kept going, and going, and going. I kept looking for the number of Ani Pema's retreat cabin as we passed various homes, yet none of the numbers of the houses matched, so we kept driving.

The road was quite steep and unpaved, and there were no turnarounds. The engineer who was driving my car was driving quite carefully so as not to gun the engine and damage the "boss's car" in any way. Meanwhile, I was becoming anxious. You could even say, truth be told, hysterical, at least on the inside. Couldn't the $%#*! engineer drive any faster? Where the $%#*! was her cabin anyway? Now we were fifteen minutes late. What if Ani Pema decided not to do the interview at all because we missed our window of opportunity?

I was furious at the engineer for driving so slowly. And I was furious at myself for directing us to drive up the wrong road. I had been to Ani Pema's cabin only a few years before; why didn't I remember where it was? Eventually, we flagged down a person near one of the homes who told us that we had to drive all the way down the steep road and then go up a different driveway about fifty yards beyond the turnoff that we had taken.

We arrived to Ani Pema's cabin about twenty-five minutes late. I, of course, apologized profusely. She commented that she hadn't even noticed.

This experience, minor as it was with no actual disastrous outcomes (in fact, far from it), prepared me perfectly for our conversation about failure. How quick I was to blame the Sounds True engineer for driving like a slow-moving turtle. How quickly I followed that with deriding myself for not having a better memory! Oh my. Imagine how distressed I can become, and others can become, when we really screw things up!

What follows is my conversation with Ani Pema about failure, about minor failures and major failures, about the perception of failure even when nothing terrible is happening, about failures in relationship and the experience of our physical body failing us, and about why Ani Pema recommends that we "fail again and fail better."

Tami Simon: In your commencement speech, you talked about how when we are in that moment of failure, many of us move to this place of blaming someone else or blaming ourselves. And I'd like to know the mechanics of how that works. In my experience, when failure happens, we suddenly feel terrible. We screwed something up. We feel all this weird sensation in our body. And the next thing you know, we're either reading someone else or ourselves the riot act about what happened. What's going on in there?

Pema Chödrön: Well, I would say that one way of describing it is that our organism is very much programmed toward seeking comfort and avoiding discomfort at any cost. At a very primitive level, we associate discomfort, which can come from feeling like we've failed, with danger, so even if the discomfort is subtle—a small discomfort—at some level our brain processes it as danger, as something to get rid of.

I feel that we as human beings need a lot of help to support us in not running away from what is unpleasant and insecure and seemingly dangerous. In other words, I would say that the drive to blame ourselves or others comes from our inability to stay present with what is, because the sense of failure challenges us. It's uncomfortable, unpleasant.

We can begin to understand that we can be with those feelings of failure—to allow those feelings—and even train ourselves to say, "I haven't done anything wrong; I'm not a bad person. I'm not a failure; I'm not a mess-up; I haven't blown it." Or, "Fundamentally, I am good, and I can allow this feeling; I can experience this feeling. I can stay with this feeling for now, maybe two seconds, or maybe four seconds, or maybe even longer."

I'm very inspired myself, as a teacher, to communicate ways to help people not run away. To help people take the view that they can allow whatever comes up, uncomfortable feelings, for example. And then secondly, to teach methods of different kinds to help others stay present.

TS: Those methods are what I'm really interested in because I think we get so immediately into "I'm a terrible person; this is my fault." When we're done blaming the other people, of course, who are coresponsible for this failure in my life, then it's "me and my fault." People are so hard on themselves, always trying to decipher how they've screwed up in the situation. So I am curious: How does somebody interrupt that tendency on the spot so that they can go back and see what's underneath?

PC: Well, first of all, underneath the whole thing always, whether we're blaming others or blaming ourselves, is this *dreadful* feeling of, "I'm not okay." No words get anywhere close to how bad that actually feels. For years now I have been curious about that feeling. And when I get into that feeling, I've noticed that it is kind of like this feeling of terrible dread that something awful is about to happen. It just feels horrible, and there isn't just one panacea. But I think *view* is very important. And by view I mean one's attitude. You have to take the view that there is nothing wrong with you; you are okay; you can allow this feeling to be there; you can "lean in to the sharp points," as Trungpa Rinpoche used to say.

This view is about turning toward instead of turning away. But that doesn't give you a method. It is about allowing yourself to be curious and finding that enthusiasm to lean in, rather than escaping the bad feelings.

It's amazing how each of us finds out for ourselves how to do these things—our own methods, so to speak. For me this is one of the greatest examples of basic goodness. That is, the question, when we are in touch with our inherent goodness, is not, "How can I get out of this awful place?" but, "How can I turn toward this? How can I lean in to this? How can I open to this?"

I also have to say that Trungpa Rinpoche never gave us one-two-three methods. The only method we got, really, was shamatha-vipassana sitting meditation, breath meditation, and tonglen practice. But there weren't step-by-step methods to get out of the bad feelings when we felt bad about ourselves or things weren't going our way. People have the wisdom to figure it out for themselves, and a lot of confidence comes from that, when you realize that you figured it out.

I've found that when I give methods, people never follow them in a one-two-three way anyway. They always make them their own. They say, "Is it alright? I kind of adapted this in this way." What do you call something where it says "one, two, three"?

TS: A recipe.

PC: A recipe, that's right. So, you give people a recipe, and it says put this much sugar and this much salt at this time and so on. And then you just don't do that at all. I want to encourage that. You just take the ingredients and do what you want. For some, however, to give recipes is good if people need a defined system to follow and just feel they shouldn't digress at all.

The first step, which is not easy to do, would be for you to become aware of what you're saying to yourself. To actually develop the ability to stand back a little bit and be aware of what you are saying to yourself in that moment of having hit bottom, having gotten to that place of dread. And it is also important to notice the story you are telling yourself.

Working with yourself in a moment of feeling failure is a bit like using meditation instruction: Be aware of your breath going in and out, stay with the feeling, and when your mind wanders off, notice that. Notice that you're thinking. And then just come back. You notice when your mind wanders off to the bad self-talk and the stories about failure, and you bring it back, just to the basic feelings.

It is the practice of noticing the difference between just being present and thinking or being distracted by thoughts. And from this ability to notice the difference comes the ability to notice what you're saying to yourself about outside circumstances.

One instruction that I give when you're in that difficult place is to notice what it is you're saying to yourself—and if it's very self-critical, if it's very harsh, don't believe what's being said. Or you can just rephrase the self-critical talk so it's more gentle and positive. In other words, you're in that place of experiencing failure and it is very difficult, and you could say, "This is really hurting, but I haven't done anything wrong." Or, "This is really painful, but I haven't done anything wrong. This pain doesn't mean that I have done anything wrong."

So a mantra you can give yourself is, "I'm okay. I haven't done anything wrong here." And at the same time acknowledge that it's really a hard place to be, or it's really a painful place to be. You can rephrase your self-talk away from, "I am a failure; I've really messed up here. I am fundamentally unlovable. I am fundamentally broken."

And oh it's so sad! So many people say, "I feel like damaged goods." I can't tell you how many times I've heard that. At the point where you feel like damaged goods and you're saying to yourself, "I am damaged goods," you can say to yourself, "Hey, wait a minute. This is really painful, but I haven't done anything wrong."

TS: Now this makes a lot of sense to me in an instance where it's a relatively small event— there was a mistake, an error, or something innocent—but there are also failures that people experience, where there's a consciousness, "You know, I *did* do something wrong."

PC: You mean like hurting someone?

TS: Yes, as in, "I acted unethically in this situation. For example, I was really interested in money instead of the other person's best interest, and it came back to haunt me, and now I feel like a failure because I actually did something wrong here."

PC: Of course, yes. This is where Western people need a lot of training, right? Because there is something cultural that reinforces the idea that we're fundamentally bad rather than basically open, fresh, full of possibilities, whole, complete—that we're basically good. So when you've actually done something intentional that hurt someone, usually what I recommend, as somebody who has been practicing the confession practice twice a month for over thirty-five years, is something like the fourth step of AA. In the fourth step, you bring forth a kind of fearless inventory of all the things that you regret having done. The idea is not to induce guilt and shame, nor is it to turn your awareness away from whatever has actually happened. It has to do with being open and honest and true about mistakes that you've made.

Once you've brought them forth, you allow yourself to feel the regret, and this becomes the method for letting the regrets go, letting them pass away. In the actual confession liturgy you say, "If acknowledged, I can lay it aside. If not acknowledged, I cannot lay it aside." It has to be acknowledged. Let the regret pierce you to the heart, and then you can lay it aside so that you don't have to carry it with you for the rest of your life as a package.

Also important is that along with the letting go, you say, "I have done something unethical, and it has harmed people, but it doesn't mean that I am basically a bad person. These qualities that caused me to do this—greed or lust or fear or aggression, whatever it was, jealousy—are temporary, removable conditions that obscure me from being in touch with my basic wholeness."

The feelings of greed and lust and so on are temporary and removable, so let's remove them. And how do you remove them? First you take the view that what's permanent in you is a basic wholeness, a basic goodness. And then the greed and fear and so on need to be acknowledged fully and laid aside—that's how they begin to dissolve. You don't want them continually coming up and luring you down that road again.

The way of no longer being a slave to these qualities isn't an act of aggression toward oneself in the sense that you say, "This part of me is bad, and I want to throw it out." There has to be some kind of understanding that to be human is to have all these different qualities; there has to be some sense of fully acknowledging these qualities. And you have to understand and trust that in and of themselves these qualities don't have to have power over you. Tibetans say the qualities no longer have your nose ring (because they used to put a ring in the nose of the yaks, and then they could pull the yak wherever they wanted).

And in fact, acknowledging your basic goodness and staying present with the feelings really works! If you are willing to not avert your eyes or tell yourself an alternate story that pretties up the picture. And if you are willing to stay present, instead of finding a kind of exit strategy that allows you not to feel, such as getting into addictions—drinking yourself into oblivion or numbing through TV or acting out through aggression. When we stay present, we feel the full extent of what it feels like to have messed up like that, to have done something that really harms somebody. Your own wisdom will show up to say, "I don't want to do that to myself anymore. I don't want to go down that road." Self-appreciation or self-kindness begins to come out. A basic new way of talking to yourself begins to emerge: "I'm fundamentally complete, and I don't need to keep obscuring myself in this way. It's so sad not only that I do this, but that everybody all over the world is doing this when the antidote to it is to learn to fully feel what it feels like to have done those things."

So the next time greed comes up, you can hear the storyline in your head that starts saying, "Well, maybe I could just, you know, cheat a little this way or slander a person a little this way, or something." Once you begin this practice of staying with the feelings, it is very different because the thoughts begin to make you feel a little sick to your stomach. On the spot, you can feel what craving feels like, you can feel what scheming feels like, you can feel what hatred feels like, you can feel what wanting revenge feels like. And whenever you stop the process and really come into the present with it and feel it, you can begin to make new and better choices for yourself.

This is some Buddhist language, but you can say, "I was born with these particular karmic propensities (jealousy, greed, or whatever it might be), and I'm going to work with them differently in this life. When these qualities get the grip on me, I'm going to do something outrageous. I'm going to stay present with them, and I'm going to train this way."

TS: Can you think of something in your own life that you would qualify as a failure? Where you feel like you'd failed in a situation. Or wish you hadn't done what you did. What did you learn from it? How did it change you?

PC: When I was in my twenties, when I had my children (my daughter was born when I was twenty-two, and my son was born when I was twenty-four), I was married, and I fell in love with somebody else. And at the time I was trying to decide whether to go with this other person or stay in the marriage with my children's father.

When I think of the amount of pain I caused around should I/shouldn't I/should I/shouldn't I, and then the amount of pain I caused by finally making the decision when I was twenty-seven to leave my first husband, to go with this other man who became my second husband, and to take the children—when I think of the amount of pain I caused by being so unconscious, unconscious about how it would impact my parents, unconscious about how it would impact my children—it can be quite difficult.

I was very conscious about how it would impact my first husband and a lot of my indecision was because I didn't want to hurt him. I didn't want to hurt him. But I never thought about my parents, I never thought about my children, if you can imagine that. I mean, it's shocking to me now. So my children were totally unprepared for suddenly getting on a train and going off with this new person that they'd only met once I think. And they were unprepared for leaving their father. They were about four and two or three and five. They were very young. I have a lot of regret about that.

While I was raising the children, I had a sort of thought of myself as the kind of archetypal good mother, earthy. We were living in Northern New Mexico with my second husband and in this era of hippie communes, which we weren't living in but we were surrounded by. I had this image of myself, but actually I was so preoccupied with my own spiritual trip, my own spiritual journey, that I was just oblivious to how it might be affecting the children.

When my second husband and I split up, I still wasn't too conscious about how all of this was impacting the children. And then I got *really* into my spiritual life and became a nun and so oblivious. And that had really quite an impact on the children. I remember my son once saying to me that when they had received my letter that I had gotten ordained as a nun—there weren't e-mails and cell phones in those days—and learned that I wouldn't be home until January instead of September, he had a dream that I came home on an airplane, but when the door to the airplane opened and I started walking out with my shaved head, some arms from inside the airplane drew me back in and closed the door. The airplane turned around and flew away. That dream of my son's was pretty powerful. I have a lot of regret about that.

One of the things is that you can't redo these kinds of things. In your mind there are therapies and things where you redo them, but I heard this interview with His Holiness the Dalai Lama, which I've talked about often in my teachings. I thought it was the optimum advice.

He was asked, "Did he have anything he regretted?" and he said yes. He had given advice to an old man that he shouldn't do certain practices because they were suited for young people and not old people. The following week the old man took his own life so that he could come back in a young body and do the practices, and the Dalai Lama felt directly responsible for the old man's death.

When asked about how he got rid of that feeling (they say he got very quiet, and he kind of went inside and closed his eyes, contacting that feeling), the Dalai Lama said, "I didn't get rid of it. The regret is still there." And he said, "You don't try to get rid of these feelings, you come to know them, and you can hold them in your heart as part of your being a human being."

Countless, countless beings share the feeling of "I wish I hadn't done that, and I have great regret that I did that." Prisons are filled with people who have that kind of deep regret for what they've done, and so is the world filled with people. The Dalai Lama could hold the regret like it was still there. He could contact the feeling of the regret, the failure, and it connected him with all humanity. It is something that all human beings feel.

Instead of failure and regret being the seed of self-loathing, it can become the seed of com-passion and empathy. The Dalai Lama also said, "I use it to spur me on to be a better person in the future, and it spurs me on more than ever to want to devote my life to helping sentient beings rather than hurting them."

I realized that it is these two things that staying with regrets offers: It can become the seed of compassion and empathy so that you can stand in the shoes of other people because you're feeling exactly what they feel. And it spurs you on to help people in the future rather than hurt them. As the Dalai Lama said, "Because otherwise, the only alternative is to have it drag you down and down and down."

Allowing yourself to get dragged down by failure builds up this huge sense of "me." "Me" as a monolithic solid, instead of a fluid, dynamic, changing process. It becomes chiseled in stone that "I am bad; I am a failure," and then you sort of get addicted to the feeling of wallowing in self-pity, wallowing in guilt and shame. And who does that help? Nobody! It doesn't help you, and it's poisonous for everybody around you. So it's a futile strategy to let failure drag you down, which we all employ rather easily.

One approach is to devote your life to helping people in the areas in which you had harmed. So, in my case, I try to bring my relationship right up in the present with the children, to have a good relationship with them now. There's nothing I can do about how I hurt my parents, but internally I review it a lot and say, "I regret that I harmed you," even though they're gone. And I also dedicate any kind of virtuous act of any kind to my parents' well-being.

When I was teaching at Omega about a year ago or so, a woman came to the mic, and she said that she worked as a social worker and she made a bad call. The bad call was that she decided that a client, who was a husband and father, was workable and okay; she decided he could stay in his home with his family. The husband had mental problems, and when he got home, he went off and killed his wife and children. When she told that story everyone's heart sort of stopped because how do you get over a feeling like that?

Someone was reminding me of that story the other day, and I remember I said something to the woman like, "You can dedicate your life to helping people in the future, rather than give up on yourself. It doesn't mean that you're funda-mentally flawed; it means you made a mistake. Obviously, it wasn't your intention to make that mistake, but you did, and it resulted in the death of these people. Whatever virtuous acts you do—the simplest of things, of being kind to someone, smiling at someone, anything—you can dedicate them to the man, to the wife, and to the children. You can be proactive in terms of helping the new people that you'll meet and also by dedicating your good acts to the family who died—keeping them in mind rather than blocking them out because it's too painful. Keep them in mind and do things to say, 'I dedicate this so that you may have well-being.'"

TS: I want to talk a little bit about your "failed" second marriage, which you referred to in the Naropa commencement speech. You talk about how it is not the reason that you became a nun. And, you know, the rumor out there—the legend, if you will—is that you wanted to kill your second husband and therefore the next step was the monastery.

PC: Oh, I see. Oh, I didn't know! [Laughs]

TS: That's the rumor, at least as I've heard it. So, why did you become a nun, if that wasn't the cause?

PC: Well, it's very interesting because, and this was right after the second marriage had ended, I was up in Northern New Mexico at Lama Foundation with my son. I was wearing a purple dress, and I was standing in a field, and I had long blonde hair, and it was blowing in the wind, and I had this kind of picture of myself as being very beautiful, you know? And Rabbi Zalman Schachter-Shalomi came up to me and said, "I just had a very clear vision of you." And I don't know what I thought he was going to say—maybe something about how he saw me as a goddess or something—who knows? And he said, "I just had this very clear vision of you as a nun standing in a cloistered garden." And I was just stunned speechless because he might as well have said, "I saw you as a tight-lipped, no sexual energy, uptight, mean-spirited, nasty person," you know? To me, his vision was not beautiful, not sensual—it was just the opposite.

It was just so insulting to me and such a shock. I think I didn't say anything; I just was speechless, because "nun" had such a negative connotation for me. I had been raised Catholic, and I had some bad experiences with nuns. So I never in my wildest dreams thought that I would become a nun. I would've done just about anything not to become a nun.

But what happened was that I became more and more interested in Buddhism. I was in England at a meditation center, where I was living for the summer. My children were with their father back in the States. I would go to this meditation center every summer, and the

Sixteenth Gyalwang Karmapa, who turned out to be a very important figure in my life, came to England, and he was offering the ordination of nuns and monks in Scotland at Samye Ling Center.

And everyone in our center (there were about thirty of us) was saying, "Should I/shouldn't I?" It just became *the* topic of the whole community. And, strange but true, I just thought, "This is forward. To become a nun is forward for me." And once I had the thought that it was forward, then not doing it was backward.

And by forward I meant, "I'm getting passionately interested in spiritual awakening, and this is forward for me; this is the method for doing it." I thought, "I don't want to get married again—that's for sure. Since the marriage broke up, I've had relationships, and they were very, very enjoyable sexual relationships, but since I don't want to get married and I can't see myself having an endless string of sexual relationships that don't lead someplace, that is no longer forward." That whole approach to my life just didn't make sense to me anymore.

And I was very young at the time—I think I was thirty-five—and I felt like I had actually completed that phase of my life. The feeling was, "I have completed that phase of my life, and forward now is symbolized by becoming a nun." Once I had that thought, there was no turning back. I had a passion for it. Later, an old lover said, "Well what did you do with all that passion?" And I said, "Well, it just got redirected naturally."

For me it was the next step. It was definitely not a choice about avoiding the pain of being left or avoiding the pain of not being loveable. It was more about making friends with all those feelings and really fully owning them and not in any way avoiding them. Becoming a nun allowed me to work everything through, almost like my full-time occupation.

TS: I'm wondering what you would say to someone who has a sense of failure in love. And they're not interested in monastic life—that wouldn't be moving forward for them. They're not interested in that choice, and they are stuck with, "I just don't think I could ever trust anybody like that again." Their relationship path, the endings, have been so painful. For some people there is a whole history of relationship failures or endings. Maybe there is a history of betrayal, something like that. What would you say to someone who has the sense that "my love life has been a failure"?

PC: Yes. Well, let me first say that though the nun's choice being for me—which was a real opening *for me*—it's a rare, rare bird where that seems like the way forward. I've met people who nun's or monk's life was a vocation for them, but they weren't coming out of my kind of situation.

So first of all (and I have had this situation with students), I'm always really interested in asking people to really look at the repeating pattern, because repeating patterns are valuable to see. If it's the situation you describe where they just keep having the same bad ending or failures to their relationships, then I say, "Your practice is going to be fully contacting that feeling you get when the relationship yet again fails."

Get deeply into contact with what it feels like to be there at the end again. And try not to jump to any conclusions like "I can never do this again," or "I'm fundamentally unlovable," or "As soon as I get close to someone, it all ends." Try to have your practice be contacting that feeling, not the storyline, and allowing yourself to really feel it.

In that feeling there is all the information you're going to need for how to unravel the repeating pattern that keeps getting you stuck. If a person works with that for a while, which is really difficult work, I say, "Okay, now why don't you get in touch with the feeling about the beginning of the relation- ship? What is at the beginning of all these relationships that hooks you, that draws you in again and again to the same kind of person? Why is it that you keep choosing the same kind of person?"

Really look at how it all gets started in the beginning. Often there's some kind of addiction or something that you're really drawn to that keeps ending with the same feeling.

Somehow this feeling at the end, as well as the feeling at the beginning of the relationship, has gotten kind of encoded in your DNA, and the way to untangle yourself from the ignorance or the confusion around it is to become very con- scious of the feeling at the end and the feeling at the beginning. It really, really helps people to not get involved again in the same pattern.

Something that's very common is that the student will get involved again, in the same kind of pattern; whatever drew them into the last five relationships, ten, or whatever, is drawing them in again. And I say, "Okay, be really aware of what you're feeling at the beginning." And of course now, because of having done this work before, there is no ignorance or bewilderment or unconsciousness. They're really aware of what's happening at the very beginning.

When they notice this, sometimes they don't go into the relationship. It helps them to choose someone different. Or sometimes they change their part of the dynamic, and then the other person doesn't want it. And sometimes they change their part of the dynamic, and it works out differently. It doesn't have that same bad ending.

TS: At the Naropa commencement ceremony you spoke on "fail, fail again, fail better." Obviously there's some kind of paradox here, or different strands of teaching. Here you're on the one hand encouraging people to fail again, and on the other hand saying to learn from our failures and not keep repeating the same patterns. Help me understand that.

PC: Well, I see it as exactly the same thing, you see. When I hear that Samuel Beckett quote, what I hear is: In your life you fail. It's just part of life that things will happen that you don't want to happen. It is part of everyone's life experience.

And it's not a one-shot deal. It happens again, right? Maybe it is a completely different scenario, but things not working out happens again because, if you're growing, if you're alive, if you really have an appetite for life— and even if you don't have an appetite for life—that's the story of anyone's life: you will meet the sense of failure.

So what I'm saying is: fail. Then fail again, and then maybe you start to work with some of the things I'm saying. And when it happens again, when things don't work out, you fail better. In other words, you are able to work with the feeling of failure instead of shoving it under the rug, blaming it on somebody else, coming up with a negative self-image—all of those futile strategies.

"Fail better" means you begin to have the ability to hold what I called in the talk "the rawness of vulnerability" in your heart, and see it as your connection with other human beings and as a part of your humanness. Failing better means when these things happen in your life, they become a source of growth, a source of forward, a source of, as I say in the talk, "out of that place of rawness you can really communicate genuinely with other people."

Your best qualities come out of that place because it's unguarded and you're not shielding yourself. Failing better means that failure becomes a rich and fertile ground instead of just another slap in the face. That's why, in the Trungpa Rinpoche story that I shared in the speech, the waves that are knocking you down begin to appear smaller and have less and less of an ability to knock you over. And actually maybe it is the same wave, maybe it's even a bigger wave than the one that hit last year, but it appears to you smaller because of your ability to swim with it or ride the wave.

And it isn't that failure doesn't still hurt. I mean, you lose people you love. All kinds of things happen that break your heart, but you can hold failure and loss as part of your human experience and that which connects you with other people.

TS: In the Naropa commencement speech, you talked about how a graduate might have the experience of looking out at the world as if he or she were stepping into a *void* or vortex that goes endlessly downward to who knows where. And whether it's a moment of graduation or some time of transition in one's life, there's this sense of being unmoored—what used to be isn't any longer. The person doesn't know what's next. That can be really terrifying for people. And I know this is something you've looked into very deeply, and you've written about a lot.

PC: Fear.

TS: Yes, and this idea of smiling at fear, to smile at fear. Please talk to me about that. I'm supposed to smile when I'm facing a void?

PC: [Laughs] One of my best friends who is not on a spiritual path—we've been really close friends since college—saw that I was doing this program called, "Smile at Fear," and she said, "Smile at fear? Give me a break, Pema!" It was like, "Barf," you know? So, I love these friends who just talk like it is.

The question actually is how to relate to fear, right? In this regard I would like to say that these transition periods where you're groundless and fearful are for the spiritual practitioner probably the most fertile ground. Because of the fact that nothing is pinned down, there are limitless possibilities right there for you if you just kind of turn your head a little bit more to the right. You can have the sense of anything is possible, as opposed to "OMG, what's going to happen to me?"

Of course that shift in attitude is facilitated greatly by having some way of relating to fear. Chögyam Trungpa Rinpoche talked a lot about fear as being a positive thing. So again, this is having an attitude that allows you to become curious about exploring something rather than just committing for life to running away from the unknown because it's so devastating or challenging.

Trungpa says that fear, unlike anger or jealousy or craving, is a very open and fluid state. It doesn't necessarily have to be narrowed down into something solid. It has a very fluid quality, which is interesting to just think about. He says loneliness is kind of the same, actually. So, fear, when it comes up, can be a moment when you say, "Oh, here's fear. This is a quality of awakened mind. This is a quality of open space." Instead of calling it groundlessness or giving it a negative name, you could just rephrase it and call it ultimate possibility, because it's unformed and open and hasn't concretized into something that makes ego feel better.

And you can also say to yourself—this is like teaching yourself the dharma on the spot— "Yes, this doesn't feel good, and yes, my knees are actually trembling, but I'm going to stay with this; I'm going to explore this; I'm interested in knowing this quality because it will take me in the direction I want to go, instead of back into the cocoon of shelter and ego-clinging."

You are offered the potential of opening up into the as-yet unknown, the much bigger world where there are smells you've never smelled, there are sights you've never seen, and there are sounds you've never heard. What you could experience is so much vaster than what you currently experience. Let's go in that direction.

TS: Given that, what would you say constitutes bravery in the face the fear? What's your definition of it?

PC: My definition of bravery in that case—or courage—would be the willingness to stay open to what you're feeling in the moment, the willingness to feel what you're feeling. We talk in the Shambhala tradition a lot about the warrior and the definition of the warrior. The warrior is one who cultivates courage and is willing to feel what he or she feels. To be completely human and be okay with being completely human, and the willingness to feel it.

TS: Sometimes from the outside people look at our lives and say, "God, that was so courageous. You did this thing; you did that thing; that was so courageous." And I know I've often had the thought, "That wasn't so courageous. If you want to know the *real* things that I did that were courageous, they are completely different."

Someone from the outside might never know what those are. So I'm curious in your life, if we were to get on the inside, what are the courageous—the really courageous—acts you've taken in your life?

PC: It would be the same thing again really—the willingness to not run away from feeling what I'm feeling when what I'm feeling is unwanted and unpleasant. And it comes up a lot now, because now I'm so committed to this path and because I see it as such a flowering or unfolding in a positive direction. I'm very committed to it.

So when I get hooked in any way or my feelings have been hurt or I feel my tendency to get obsessive, which is one of my qualities, or I want to really tell somebody off, any of those things where there's that strong pull to go in an old, habitual, small-minded kind of direction, then the courage is to not heed the call of the sirens in that particular moment, but to just stay present and feel what I'm feeling.

Every time I do it, I think, "Oh my gosh, how can I be asking people to do this? Because this is actually very difficult." It's humbling every single time, and it fills me with awe when I realize that other people are actually doing this, because it does take a lot of courage and bravery.

I think any of these things where we have a habitual pattern and then we interrupt that habitual pattern through gentleness or through kindness takes a lot of courage.

TS: One other question, Ani Pema, about fear. Especially when we look at what might be holding us back from taking a risk in our life—a risk to write the book I really want to write, or a risk to try a new career or whatever—is this fear of potentially being criticized by other people. Other people are going to think terrible things about me if I put myself out in this way and I'm not well received. This fear of criticism is one of the things that keeps people back, and I wonder if you can help people with that.

PC: [Chuckles] Well, first I can say, it's going to happen. You write a book, and of course there is going to be a lot of criticism. It is all right out there, you know, in black and white on the paper or on the computer. There it is for people to see and pick apart. And all I can say is, "If you follow your heart, you're gonna feel better than if you hold back because of fear."

But when you follow your heart—with a career change, or writing the book, or whatever it might be—there is no guarantee that the whole thing won't be a total failure, and there's no guarantee that you're not going to get criticisms. You'll get praise *and* blame is the usual scenario. And you just want to hear the praise and don't want to hear the blame.

The question is, are you going to grow or are you going to just stay as you are out of fear and waste your precious human life by status quo-ing instead of being willing to break the sound barrier? Break the glass ceiling, or whatever it is in your own life? Are you willing to go forward?

I suggest finding the willingness to go forward instead of staying still, which is essentially going backward, particularly when you have a calling in some direction. That calling needs to be answered. And it's not necessarily going to work out the way you want it to work out, but it is taking you forward, and you are leaving the nest. And that never can be a mistake—to fly instead of staying in the nest with all the poop and everything that's in there.

TS: What if someone says, "You know, I'm paralyzed by fear. I hear what you're saying, and

I agree with what you're saying. I want to follow my calling. I want to, but I have this feeling of just too much terror."

PC: I'd say to be really gentle with yourself, to not push it, and to just move toward it slowly for the next five years and the next ten years. Just keep making baby steps, moving toward the fear, and part of that will be just working with fear, through meditation, for example.

Be gentle, go slow, take your time—but keep your eye on the goal, as they say. Say, "This is something I want to do, I'm going to move toward it, and I have an end date, which could be in a year, or in two years, three years, five, ten." If you are really paralyzed with fear, really to that degree, which I know many of us are, give yourself the time. Give yourself enough time so your stomach can unknot when you think about doing it.

And in the meantime, you've got to keep your eye on that goal and start moving toward it, working with the fear, and doing the other things that might help you change careers or write the book or whatever. If it's something like writing, just start—don't not write the book. You could just start keeping a blog, or keep a journal. Keep moving in the direction you want to go.

TS: Now the last area of conversation about failure that I want to talk about has to do with a feeling I think that very many people have at some point in their life, that their body is failing them.

PC: Oh, yes. I know that one.

TS: And it can be quite, quite painful, this sense of "my body doesn't give me the support it used to," whether that's through the aging process or an illness. How can you help people work with that sense of failure?

PC: You know there have been many beautiful books written about people whose bodies just gave out on them or who had chronic pain or something, and about how they turned that into their path.

First of all, I know a little about this myself because I'm nearing eighty and I have all kinds of physical things. It's like what Leonard Cohen says, "I ache in the places where I used to play." But in terms of aging—getting older—that's just one thing; that's different from an illness that happens to you when you're younger. In terms of aging, there is no reason to get so bent out of shape and upset about getting older. I mean, we've been warned, right? If you're a spiritual person, you've been warned over and over that one of the sufferings is old age and sickness, and that it is followed by death. Even if you're not a spiritual person, you've seen all these old people. What made you think it wasn't going to happen to you?

You might have kidded yourself all along, but now that it's happening, how about saying, "Well, this is just natural. If there's anything that's a natural part of being a human being it's that the machine starts wearing out, and eventually I'm going to die." Try to not make it out to be such a dreadful thing to age or to die. That's easier said than done, but I can say this to you as someone who's aging. When I think about being eighty years old, I remember no one in my family ever lived past eighty-five, and I think, whoa. That's not the kind of time that passes with a finger snap, you know? So to not see aging as a problem seems quite important to me.

And I'll tell you: spirit is everything. I watched this interview that Oprah Winfrey did with her mentor, Maya Angelou, and Maya Angelou—who died I think at eighty-six—was at the time about eighty-five, and Oprah Winfrey asked her, "Well, how do you feel about, you know, being eighty-five?"

And she said, "If you get a chance, do it." And I just loved that! If you get a chance, do it! That's attitude. Attitude is everything, and boy, what a difference it makes!

I can see why we're encouraged as practitioners to practice and establish good habits of meditation when you're younger, because it doesn't get easier when you're older. Sometimes you have to start taking medications that really make it harder to not get distracted and to just keep your mind open and in one place. I can't just sit down and meditate for an hour, half an hour even, anymore. I have to get up and move, because there are these things that make sitting more complicated.

TS: And you have to do that because of pain?

PC: I have a bad back, yes. So it does get tougher when you get older, but you should expect that that can happen. Keep that in mind when you're younger. Don't just think, "Well, when I get older, and I can retire, then it's going to be easy," because it could be harder. That's a little digression, but I wanted to add that.

Now that old age is happening, it's like, gosh, I look at someone in a walker and I feel such empathy for them and compassion for the situation. I think, you know, that could be me tomorrow walking around like that, shuffling along with a walker. The machine starts giving out, and so your spirit is everything at that point, and your attitude.

If you're young and then suddenly you suffer an accident or illness, something that is coming out of the blue and it's not part of the natural process of a human life unfolding, again, attitude is everything. I can say from having had chronic fatigue for over twenty years, attitude is everything. And we have these famous examples of people, such as Stephen Hawking, who can't move anything. He's such an example of how life goes on, how you can still live an inspiring and inspired life when you have the worst of disabilities. Feeling sorry for yourself or obsessing with all the storylines, which are kinds of disaster scenarios, is a very common thing. With chronic fatigue, I was fortunate to be a meditation practitioner because I never developed depression around having chronic fatigue, and developing depression during an illness is quite common.

Part of the thing that people have a hard time coming to terms with when they are ill isn't the illness itself. For example, high achievers who get chronic fatigue might feel they can't be who they used to be in their own eyes, or in other people's eyes, and this can be very difficult. It's so heartbreaking, and it damages your ego, and that's why people get depressed. But there's no need for that, really. There's just no need for that if you're just living moment-to-moment, without the storyline about what an illness means about you as a human being or what other people are going to think of you.

Chronic fatigue doesn't have extreme pain, but now that I have back pain, I can say that chronic fatigue was a lot worse than back pain, which sometimes comes with pretty severe pain. With chronic fatigue you just feel lousy all the time. You have no chi; you have no life-force energy. You can hardly lift your hand. And people say, "But you look so good." And it doesn't matter what you look like; you just feel horrible all the time. You feel like you're coming down with the flu twenty-four hours, seven days a week, all year long, year after year after year. In this case, and in the case of any illness, you don't need to believe the storylines that you tell yourself about who you are and the fear of what other people are going to think of you. Instead you can accept that there's nothing wrong with you; you're still a whole, complete person.

I've been doing a practice with a lot of my students lately of recognizing our wholeness. Recognize your wholeness, just as you are—complete just as you are. Some of my students say they use it like a mantra when something happens that generates fear or pain or anything that causes the mind to twist into "I am a failure, I am bad, my life is over."

In those moments, they say to themselves, "This moment is complete just as it is; I'm complete just as I am; things are whole and fine just as they are." It allows you somehow to just relax with the situation as being complete just as it is, rather than to follow your spin on it that something's wrong, you've done something wrong, or something wrong has happened.

And of course it feels like something wrong has happened when you wake up after the accident and you're paralyzed from the neck down or something. I can only imagine what that puts you through. But at some point, having gone through some kind of grieving process and feeling really, really wretched, you can just say, "I haven't done anything wrong. My true nature has not been touched by this. Who I really am is still the same as before."

Whether it's a mental illness or physical disability, it hasn't touched your basic nature. You can trust that and come back to that as a touchstone. And so the practice always, again and again, is to be able to feel what you feel without this spinoff of storyline that you tell yourself about it, but to stay with it just as it is with a lot of gentleness and even appreciation.

TS: You said this beautiful line in talking about the aging process that "spirit is everything."

PC: Spirit *is* everything.

TS: What do you mean by that?

PC: I guess another way to say it is attitude is everything. Attitude with a kind of *lungta,* which means uplifted, connected with the energy of life. It's seeing the glass half-full. And there's a potential for growth always in whatever is happening.

This doesn't mean feeling good or feeling bad, but going beyond those labels of good and bad. You can experience your true nature as vast, open, fresh, unbiased, and not caught up in these labels that we pin on things.

Spirit is everything in terms of the aging process. Looking at things as positive, something forward—let's use the word forward instead of positive, because that includes whatever might happen. Instead of going backward into trying to find these little islands of security that keep giving out on you, you learn instead to fly or float and be okay in the formlessness or the groundlessness or the open-endedness of things, which is who you truly have been all along.

You never really know what is going to happen next, and you never know who you are from moment to moment. It's all completely unfolding. You see, for myself at this stage, it's just thrilling how it just keeps unfolding. Even boredom unfolds.

TS: Forward.

PC: Forward! That's our motto.

TS: Beautiful. Thank you, Ani Pema.

ABOUT THE AUTHOR

Pema Chödrön is the author of many spiritual classics including *When Things Fall Apart, The Places That Scare You, Taking the Leap,* and *Living Beautifully.* She serves as resident teacher at Gampo Abbey Monastery in Nova Scotia and is a student of the late Chögyam Trungpa Rinpoche, Dzigar Kongtrül Rinpoche, and Sakyong Mipham Rinpoche.